The Gospel Explained in Simple Drawings

The Good News can be clearly understood

By Dr. Douglas Hammett

ISBN: 978-0-86645-295-3

You can get the first lesson in the Gospel Lessons by contacting
Bible Baptist Ministries
On Whatsapp: +27-711-222706
On Facebook: http://www.Facebook.com/BibleBapMin
By Email: BibleStudyAfrica@gmail.com

Table of Contents

Lesson One
Are You Ready for Your Appointment?
Hebrews 9:27

This is a book on drawing the Gospel. These are short scripture diagrams, pictures illustrating Bible verses.

We are going to look at some very key Bible truths that you need to understand about the Gospel of Jesus Christ.

Hebrews 9:27 says, ***"And as it is appointed unto man once to die, but after this the judgment."***

My question for you today is, are you ready for your appointment? Yes, all of us have an appointment.

The Bible says in Hebrews 9:27, *"And as it is appointed."* The word appointed means you have an appointment. You have a meeting that has been scheduled.

But you have not made that appointment. Someone else has made that appointment for you.

According to the Word of God, the person who has made that appointment, who has set the number of the days that you will be alive, is God Himself. You have an appointment made by God.

"And as it is appointed unto man." It is an appoint for all of mankind—men and woman. All of mankind have an appointment.

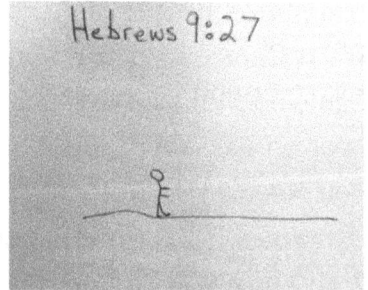

4

"And as it is appointed unto man once to die." All of us are going to die. No matter who we are, we cannot escape death.

Do you know what day you will die? Do you know how long in life you have left?

No person on earth knows how long it will be before they die. Only God knows that.

Hebrews 9:27

Long ago, when I was a young man, my father passed away. For the first time I began to consider that one day I too would die.

I was concerned. Where had my father gone?

I was probably even more concerned about myself. When am I going to die, and what will it be like for me on the other side of death?

Those questions plagued me. They bothered me. They became the worry of my mind.

I began to look to others to try to find the answer to my questions. But I found the answer in the Word of God.

The Bible says, *"It is appointed unto man once to die."* You and I will only die one time. We are not coming back for another chance.

Some people believe when you die that you will go in the grave and stay there. That is not what the Word of God teaches.

The Bible says, *"And as it is appointed unto man once to die, but after this the judgment."*

What is judgment? If you commit a crime, you will have to stand before the judge and give an answer for why you did it. The judge will assign your punishment.

All men are going to die. All men will then stand before Almighty God and give an answer to God for their life.

Romans 14:12, *"So then every one of us shall give account of himself to God."* You will answer to God for everything you have done. My guess is that you do not remember everything that you have done.

You do not remember every good thing you have done, and you do not remember every sin that you have committed.

You will stand before Almighty God and give an account for everything, even the things that you do not remember.

God will not be like the judges of this earth. The Bible says, in Romans 2:2 that God will judge *"according to truth."*

You and I will be judged according to the truth of what has gone on in our life, and according to the truth of the Word of God itself.

What is truth? men ask. Men will try to change their words and change their stories, but God knows what the truth is.

In Romans 2:16, we are told that God will judge every secret of man. Every person on earth has secrets.

There are things about my life I will not tell you. There are things about your life that you will not tell me. There are things in our lives that we try to keep hidden from everybody else.

The truth is, God knows every single secret, and every secret will be brought to light in that day of judgment.

You have an appointment. You do not know when that appointment is going to happen, but when it does, you will then stand before God.

He will judge you according to the truth.

You will not be able to bribe Him or argue with Him. You will not be able to corrupt Him. He will judge you according to the truth.

You will answer for every deed done in your life. You will answer even for the secrets that you have hidden from everyone else.

When you stand before God, you will be judged according to the truth.

John 17:17 tells us, *"Thy word is truth."* It is the Word of God that is truth.

If you want to know what the truth is that God will judge you by, then you need to know the Word of God.

7

If you want to be ready to answer in that day, you need to know the Bible and God's answer.

The truth is all of us have sinned. The truth is all of us will stand before God in judgment.

The truth is there is a way to be ready for that day of judgment, that day of giving an account, that day of examination of your life.

You need to be ready. Let me encourage you to prepare by hearing what God has to say in the Word of God about that judgment.

Lesson Two
Did God Really Mean That?
Romans 3:23

In this chapter, we are going to look at Romans 3:23. We are going to ask the question, "Did God really mean that?"

In Romans 3:23, the Bible says, *"For all have sinned and come short of the glory of God."*

What does it mean to sin? There are two words that are most often used in the Bible for the word **sin.**

The first word talks about a trespass, to step across the line. For example, if you enter someone's property where you do not belong, you are trespassing. You stepped onto their land.

The second word is the word that means to miss the mark. That is the word that is used here in this verse.

It is the idea of having a target that you are shooting at with a bow and arrow, and you want to hit that target right in the very middle.

Not everyone hits the target. In fact, we often miss. We will shoot the arrow, but it does not hit the target.

You have heard of the Ten Commandments in the Bible. God wrote them on the tablets of stone and gave them to Moses.

9

The first four commandments have to do with our relationship with God. We know God desires to have a relationship with us.

If we are going to have a relationship with God, He expects us to live a holy life, a life without sin. The Bible says that we are to be perfect as our Father in heaven is perfect. The question is, "Have you sinned?"

God says in Romans 3:23, *"All have sinned."* That includes everyone who lives in this world. So let's think about those Ten Commandments. How well are we keeping them?

The first commandment, number one, God says, *"Thou shalt have no other gods before me."*

What is God saying? He's saying, "I want you to keep Me first in everything you do." In everything you do, consider Me first. In everything you do, think of Me first. In every decision you make, consider Me first."

Could I ask you the question: do you do everything for God and only God? Do you make every decision according to His will and not your will?

Well, we all know the answer to that! I have often made decisions for myself. I have chosen to do the things that I wanted instead of the things that God wanted.

I have broken God's law. I have missed the mark; I did not hit the bullseye of perfection. I am not perfect. I have not always loved God. I have not always put God first.

Romans 3:23
Sinned - miss. MARK

Yes, there are times when I have, but many times, I have chosen myself over God. I have put myself first, and therefore, I have broken the first commandment.

The second commandment, found in Exodus 20:4-5, says that we are not to bow down before idols.

No idols. An idol is something or someone that you put before God. An idol in the Bible is someone or something that you serve in place of God.

Anything or anyone that you would rather have instead of God, if you choose them ahead of God, that is an idol. Is there any person that you want more than God?

Maybe if you are a man reading this, it might be a woman that you want more than you want God. You would even sin against God to get that woman.

Or maybe as a woman, there is a man that you wish that you had. You would rather have that man than have the will of God, and you are willing to sin to get that man.

For a thief, he wants the money that he is stealing or the cellphone that he is taking more than he wants God. He has broken the second commandment.

The things of this earth--money, people, a car, a job, your children-- all these things can become an idol. Anything that you love more than you love God becomes an idol.

If we are honest, we must all admit that many times we love things in our life more than we love God. We have broken the second commandment. We have missed the mark.

Romans 3:23
Sinned - miss. mark

The third commandment, we also break. This commandment says, *"Thou shalt not take the name of the LORD thy God in vain."*

The word vain speaks of taking the name of God in an empty way. To use God's name as if it did not matter.

Now, that could be something as serious as taking God's name and cursing with His name.

Asking God to damn someone or damn something--that is taking God's name in an empty way. It definitely is blasphemy, and it is breaking that third commandment.

Have you ever done that? Even if you have not done that, have you ever stood in church and sung a song to God, but your mind was not thinking about what you were singing?

Maybe while you were singing, you were thinking about what you were going to do after church was over? Indeed, you were singing in the name of God, but not thinking anything about God.

That is what the word vain means. It means to sing emptily, or to talk in an empty way about God, to not have your mind and your heart set fully upon God. That, my friend, is breaking the third commandment.

Romans 3:23
Sinned - miss mark
VAIN

The fourth commandment is the commandment that says, *"Remember the sabbath day, to keep it holy."*

The Sabbath day was given to the nation of Israel. It was a day set aside to remember God.

This is the only commandment that is not repeated in the New Testament. But the idea of giving God time and honoring Him is repeated in the New Testament.

The Apostle Paul tells us in Romans 14:5 that one man may esteem or value one day above another. But another man can esteem, or value, every day alike. But every man be fully persuaded in his own mind.

Whether we give God one day a week, or whether we set time aside all through the week for God, we owe to God time.

We owe to God our life. We owe to God our attention. We owe God everything we have.

The truth is, when I go back and think about this, there have been many days that I have not given God the time that He rightly deserves. I have broken the fourth commandment.

There have been many times when I have used God's name in vain-- as I have been singing or talking about God, but not truly thinking about God. That is a violation of the third commandment.

There have been times when I have chosen things over God. There have been times when I have chosen people who I wanted to be with more than I wanted to be with God. That is a violation of the second commandment.

There have been times when God has definitely not been first in my life. I have broken the first commandment.

I have broken all four of these commandments. I am guilty of breaking the law. I am guilty before Almighty God.

Now, here is the good news. All have sinned; all have missed the mark. I have missed the mark; you have missed the mark.

God does not tell us we have missed the mark because He wants to make us feel bad and leave us there.

God tells us about our sin so we can find out that we have a problem. But He also has a solution. We need to get the answer that only God can give us.

Did God really mean that? Has God told us the truth? Yes, He has. All have sinned. All have missed the mark.

All of us are not right with God until we come to Him the Bible way, through Jesus Christ.

Sin is missing the mark, not doing what God has told us we need to do.

We have all broken those commandments, and we are guilty before Almighty God.

Lesson Three
How Do You Measure Up?
Romans 3:23

In this chapter, we want to look at the question, "How do you measure up against God's Word?"

We want to go back to Romans 3:23. In the last chapter, we looked at this verse a little bit.

The Bible says in Romans 3:23, *"For all have sinned, and come short of the glory of God."*

The word **sin** means to miss the mark. It is like shooting an arrow at a target, trying to hit the center bullseye. But instead, the arrow goes off to the side.

You do not hit the target. You miss the mark. That is what the Bible says about us.

We have sinned. We have lived our lives in a wrong way. We should honor God with all of our heart, every moment of every day that we live. But we have missed that mark.

We have not honored God every day. We have not honored God every moment of every day. We have missed the mark.

We have also taken God's name in vain. We have taken His name and used it in an empty way. We have not used it in honor and great respect all the time.

If you break those commandments just one time, you are guilty of missing the mark. To sin means to miss the mark.

But this verse says, ***"All have sinned, and come short of the glory of God."*** How do we come short of God's glory?

The word **glory** means honor. It means to lift God up; to raise Him up so all can see Him for who He is.

The Bible says in Genesis 1 that all men were made in the image of God and after His likeness.

We were made for the purpose of bringing honor and glory to God. We do that by the way we live, by the way we talk, and by the way we think.

This is why we are told in the New Testament that in everything we do, we are to do it all to the glory of God. Everything we do should be to bring glory to God.

Yet, the truth is that when we measure ourselves according to God's law, we miss the mark, and we come short of the glory of God. We do not measure up.

Think about it this way. When God gave the Ten Commandments to Moses, there were two tables of stone.

The first one dealt with our responsibility to God. There were

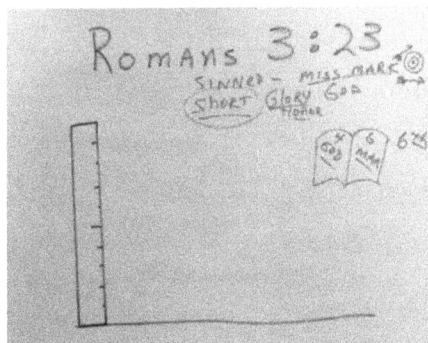

four commandments on that tablet. We looked at those commandments in our last lesson.

The second tablet dealt with our responsibility to mankind. There were six commandments on that tablet.

We do not have time today to look at all six commandments but let me just mention a few of them.

First of all, the sixth commandment says that, *"Thou shalt not kill."* The word kill means to murder, to kill someone.

If I ask most people, "Have you committed murder? Have you killed someone?" Most people say, "No."

The truth is, most people have not. Some have, but there is even hope for those who have.

In the Bible, we do find people who have committed murder. Moses committed murder. The Apostle Paul became a murderer.

But if you are saying, "I've never committed murder," listen to the words of Jesus.

He says in Matthew 5:21-22, *"Ye have heard that it was said by them of old time, Thou shalt not kill; and whosoever shall kill shall be in danger of the judgment; But I say unto you, That whosoever is angry with his brother without a cause shall be in danger of the judgment."*

You do not have to put a knife into someone and kill them in order to break this commandment. All you need to do is be angry with a person.

How about you? I have never killed anyone. But according to the definition of Jesus Christ who will be the judge on that day, if I have ever been angry with anyone, I am guilty of breaking this commandment.

When I look at my life, I do not measure up to the perfection that God wants me to. I do not go all the way to the top. I have come short.

This is how men are. We have broken the law of God.

The seventh commandment says, *"Thou shalt not commit adultery."*

Many people say, "I have never slept with another woman or another man besides my spouse."

The Bible defines adultery differently, however, than we do. Look at what Jesus said about adultery.

In Matthew 5:27, Jesus says: *"Ye have heard that it was said by them of old time, Thou shalt not commit adultery: But I say unto you, That whosoever looketh on a woman to lust after her hath committed adultery with her already in his heart."*

All you need to do is look at a woman and to think of her in a sexual way, and you have broken the seventh commandment. You have come short of the glory of God.

It does not matter whether she is married or not. To simply look at a woman that is not your wife and to think of her in an immoral way is breaking this commandment.

When I look at my life, I do not measure up to the perfection that God wants me to. I do not go all the way to the top. I have come short.

How about you? Do you measure up or do you come short?

The eighth commandment says to us, *"Thou shalt not steal."* Stealing is simply taking something that does not belong to you. It could be something large like stealing a car.

But it could be something small, like taking someone's cellphone or even taking a piece of paper without asking or stealing a little bit of food from someone when they are not looking.

That is breaking the eighth commandment. It is coming short of the glory of God. It is not living up to all that God wants you to live up to in order to bring honor and glory to Him.

As I look at my life, I see that I have not measured up to what God wants. I have broken His commandments and I am guilty before God. How about you? How do you measure up?

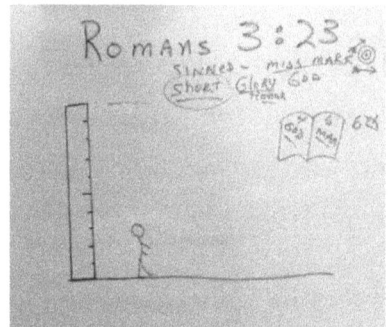

The Bible says, *"All have sinned."* It does not matter whether it is you or me. I have broken the law; you have broken the law. All have come short of the glory of God.

If you ask the question, "Is there anyone who has ever lived up to all that God wants?" I would say to you, "Yes, there is."

There is one person who has lived in such a manner that He has shown the glory of God. His name is the Lord Jesus Christ.

Jesus lived in this life without any sin. He never did sin. He never spoke sin. He never even thought sin.

There was no sin in His life at any time. There is not one of the Ten Commandments that Jesus ever broke.

When you and I measure ourselves against the law of God, we come up short. We do not measure up.

When we measure ourselves next to the Lord Jesus Christ, we realize that we have not perfectly given glory to God the Father.

There is a remedy. Some people believe that the law is the way to made right with God, but they misunderstand the purpose of the law.

Why did God give us the law? He did not give us the commandments in order that we would be able to keep them to get into heaven. We are going to talk about that in the very next chapter.

21

But for now, I want you to see that all men are sinners. It does not matter who you are, it does not matter what your race or nationality is.

All men everywhere have sinned and broken the law of God. We have missed the mark, and we have come short of the glory of God.

Therefore, we need Jesus Christ. We need a Savior to rescue us from our sin.

Lesson Four
Two Mistakes People Make with the Law of God
Romans 3:20

We are going to look at Romans 3:20. I want you to see two mistakes that people make with the law of God.

These two mistakes are important to know to understand the way of God and the real purpose of God's law in the Bible. Most people make these two mistakes.

Romans 3:20, *"Therefore by the deeds of the law there shall no flesh be justified in his sight: for by the law is the knowledge of sin."*

What is he talking about? What is the knowledge of sin?

The Bible says that the purpose of God's law is to give us understanding and to help us know that we have a problem with sin. God's law helps us to be able to see our sin when otherwise we may not have been able to see it or understand it.

The first mistake that most people make with the law of God is this: they claim ignorance. *They think that if they do not know what the law is, God will say they are innocent.*

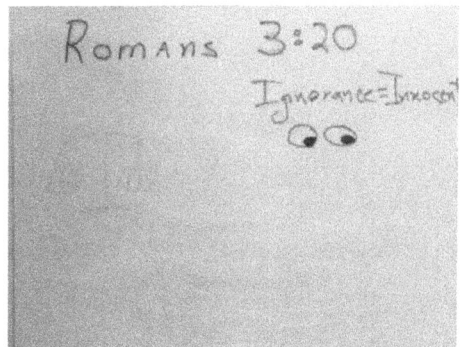

Romans 3:20
Ignorance = Innocent

Recently, I was driving on a new road that I have not been on before. As I was on that road driving, I

23

saw the sign that said 100 kilometers. I was driving about 90 kilometers an hour, well under the speed limit.

I came over the hill, and there were police. When they saw my car, they pulled me over and they asked me, "Do you know why we stopped you? It is because you were speeding."

I said, "I saw a sign. It said 100. I was not going that fast."

The lady police officer said, "There was another sign that said 80."

I had not seen that sign and I told her so. Do you know what she did? She wrote me a ticket. She did not believe me.

I did not know what the speed limit was. I thought it was 100. Most people say, "If you do not know (ignorance) then that means you are innocent."

That lady police officer would not let me go. She did not say I was innocent. No, she said I was guilty because I should have seen that sign.

When you and I look at the law of God, it informs us. It teaches us. It explains to us what sin is.

We could look at any of the Ten Commandments and see that we have a problem. We have broken God's law.

For instance, in the last lesson we looked at the sixth commandment that says, *"Thou shalt not kill."* Jesus tells us that if we are angry with our brother, we have broken this commandment.

Now, you may not have ever killed anyone, but I am sure that you have been angry with someone in your life. The Bible says you are guilty before God.

The seventh commandment says, *"Thou shalt not commit adultery."* Maybe you have never slept with your neighbor's wife. Maybe you have never been with your neighbor's husband.

But the Bible says that if you look with lust in your heart upon another person, you desire to have them sexually, then you are guilty of breaking this law.

We have just looked at two of the commandments. God's laws show us that we are guilty. They explain to us that we are guilty before God, and we do have a problem.

That's the first mistake that most people make with God's law. They think if they do not know what the law is, that God will say they are innocent.

But God says, "No, you are guilty because you have broken these laws, and you should know what those laws are and understand what I require." God gave us the Word of God so we could know His laws.

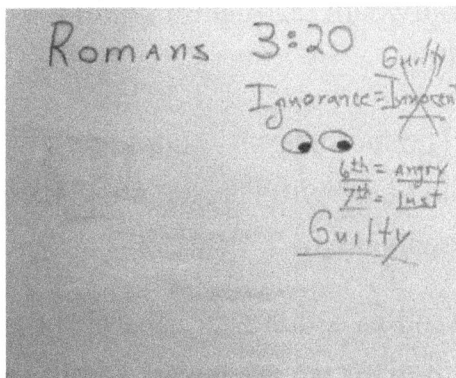

There's a second mistake that is often made by people. ***They believe that somehow the law will make them right with God.*** They think the law's purpose, the reason it was given, was to make them right.

Look again at Romans 3:20, *"Therefore, by the deeds of the law there shall no flesh be justified in his sight."*

The *deeds of the law* is talking about the works you do to keep the law, to obey the law. Paul says that no person, not one man, shall be justified in that way.

To be *justified* means to be made right. Most people think that the law was given to make us right.

But Romans 3:20 says the law was not given to justify us. No person, no flesh will be made right by keeping the law of God.

Most people believe that somehow keeping the law will make them right with God. They think, "If I do enough good things in my life, they will outweigh the bad things in my life."

The lie that most people believe is this: I will be able to get better, and God will forgive me. Therefore, if I do enough good, it will take away the bad.

God says that is not the purpose of the law. The law's purpose is to show us we are guilty, not to make us right.

When the police officer gave me the ticket for speeding, what if I had said, "Can I go back and drive this road again and drive the speed limit? Then will you let me go?"

She would have said, "No, you have already broken the law. You are guilty before the law of South Africa, and you must pay the fine."

What if I drive over the road 100 times, and I obey the law every time, and I only break the law one time? She would say, "You still must pay the fine."

This is exactly what James 2:10 tells us. The Bible says there, *"Whosoever shall keep the whole law, and yet offend in one point, he is guilty of all."*

You may obey the whole law over and over and over again. Yet if one time you break one law of God, you are guilty.

This is how God looks at your sin and mine. He sees us as guilty. The law's purpose is to help us see how guilty we are before God.

The law cannot clean us up. The law cannot make us right. The only way to be made right is for the payment for our sin to be made.

That's why the Gospel is so important. The law cannot save you. You cannot live good enough to go to heaven because the Bible tells us, *"All have sinned."*

I have sinned. You have sinned. Every man on earth has sinned. We need a Savior. The law does not make you innocent because you do not know about it. You are still guilty.

27

The law can never make you right with God. The purpose of the law is to show you that you are guilty so that you will listen to God's remedy.

Lesson Five
What Choice Will You Make?
Romans 6:23

Now we want to consider the question, "Have you made your choice?" In Romans 6:23, we are going to be talking about the choice that God has placed before every person on this earth.

Romans 6:23, *"For the wages of sin is death; but the gift of God is eternal life through Jesus Christ our Lord."*

In Romans 3:23, God tells us, *"All have sinned."* We understand that every man will stand before Almighty God and answer for his own life. We must be prepared for that day of judgment.

The Bible says that when Adam originally sinned, he faced death. He not only had physical death that eventually came to him, but he had spiritual death that happened the moment that he committed sin.

That spiritual death separated him from Almighty God.

In Romans 6:23, God tells us that the wages of the sin that we commit is death. One day each one of us will die physically.

No matter what you try to do or think about, death is on its way, coming after you. It's got you by the foot, ready to pull you into the grave at any moment.

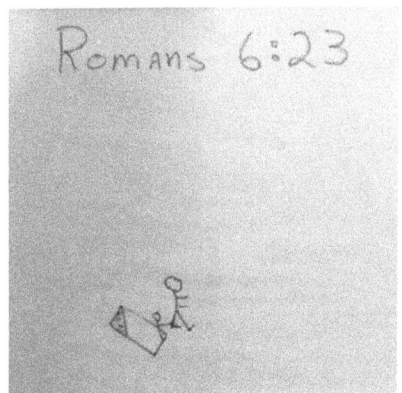

If you look around, you will find people around you are dying all the time. Funeral homes are very busy.

As I look back in my life, very early in my life my father passed away. Death came my direction.

I began to wonder what would happen after I die. I realized that death was coming my way, and I needed to make preparation.

In this verse, Romans 6:23, the Bible says, *"The wages of sin is death."*

Wages are a paycheck. God tells us that there is something that we are going to earn by our sinning.

When you and I choose to disobey God, we are choosing to increase our wages, to increase our paycheck. We are choosing to earn more because of our sin.

The Bible says, *"The wages of sin is death."* When we sin, we are choosing death.

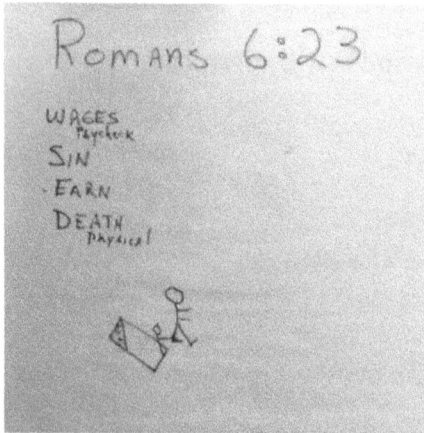

In the Bible there are two kinds of death. There is physical death, which all of us are going to face. We have a grave that is pulling us in. Death is on its way.

But there is also a spiritual death, a separation from Almighty God; a separation that keeps us apart from God.

God, on the other hand, is waiting for us, offering to us eternal life. He is offering to us forgiveness of sins. He is making this offer.

"The gift of God is eternal life." It is a free gift.

Eternal life is a relationship that we have with God right now in this life. Eternal life is also in eternity when we die and go to heaven to be with God.

Now, notice what we are learning here in this verse. The wages, the paycheck that we deserve and we have earned from our sin, is death.

That death is what comes upon all men. Physical death shows us that indeed we are sinners and there is a judgment coming.

But the greater death we need to be concerned about is that spiritual death that causes a barrier between us and God. Spiritual death is eternal separation from God.

God offers to us a gift. This gift comes from God, and it is something that is given to us freely.

It is free to us, but it costs God something to give us this life. It cost God the life of His only begotten Son, the Lord Jesus Christ.

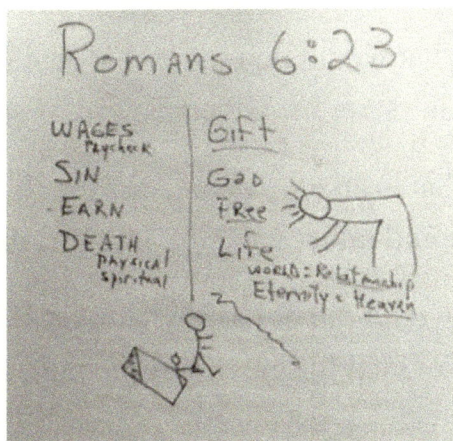

This life that God offers to us is an eternal life, which gives us a relationship with Him and eventually a home in heaven when we die.

Sometimes people are asked the question, "Can you know when you die you are going to go to heaven?" The answer most people give is no.

The reason they say that is because they know that there is a paycheck coming that they deserve, and it is spiritual death, separation from God for all of eternity.

But the Bible teaches that there is a gift that you can receive. So, is it possible for a person to know that they have received the gift of God? The answer is absolutely yes.

There is a difference between choosing to get your wages, your paycheck, and choosing to take the gift of God.

What would you rather have: spiritual death which is hell, or would you rather have the free gift of spiritual life, which is heaven?

That is an easy choice for me to make. I would rather have heaven. I would rather have the free gift that God offers.

I would rather have what God is offering to me than what Satan has provided for me. I deserve hell. I deserve judgment. I deserve the paycheck for my sin.

Yet God has made a way for me to receive the free gift that He has already paid for. He offers to give me eternal life, a relationship with Him and a place in heaven.

The choice is mine. Which will I choose?

Which choice would you prefer? The choice of death and hell, or life and eternity in heaven?

Which will you choose?

Lesson Six
Can God Make a Way?
Genesis 22:8 - Abraham and Isaac

In this chapter, we are going to look at the story of Abraham and Isaac. God was testing Abraham to see if he was willing to obey God.

In Genesis 22:8, the Bible says, *"And Abraham said, My son, God will provide himself a lamb for a burnt offering: so they went both of them together."*

God had given directions to Abraham that he was to go up to the mountain and he was to take his son Isaac with him.

Abraham was walking towards the mountain with his son Isaac. Abraham was about 120 years old. His son was about 30 years of age.

As they were going up to the mountain, the Bible says that Isaac looked, and he saw that they had wood for a fire. They had the fire to start the wood to burn the offering, but they had no animal to offer as a sacrifice.

So Isaac said, "Father, where is the lamb?" Abraham answered with these words, "My son, God will provide himself a lamb." God will do the providing.

When they got to the mountain, they built there an altar on the mountain for a sacrifice to be made. They prepared that altar, and then Abraham did what God had told him.

Genesis 22:8
sentence = death

He bound up his son, his only son Isaac, and he put Isaac on that altar. Abraham prepared to do what God had told him to do--to kill his only son and offer him as a sacrifice.

God had given to Abraham the message that he was to take his son Isaac up to mountain because his son had a sentence of death upon his life. God had said that Isaac is going to die.

Yes, God had said there is a sentence of death upon Isaac, but God had also made a promise.

That promise was that Isaac was going to live, and that through Isaac, Abraham's only son by Sarah, he would have children, who in turn would have more children and become a great nation, a very large nation. God had given the promise of life.

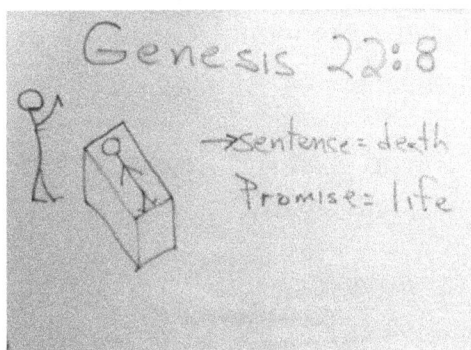
Genesis 22:8
→ sentence = death
Promise = life

We have the sentence of death and the promise of life. Can God make a way? How can Isaac live and yet die at the same time? God began to make a way.

35

God told Abraham to lift up his eyes and look over in the bushes, There he would find a ram, a lamb, that would be waiting for him.

Abraham found this lamb, and that lamb was God's provision for Isaac to be able to live. God gave a substitute. God provided the lamb so that Isaac could live.

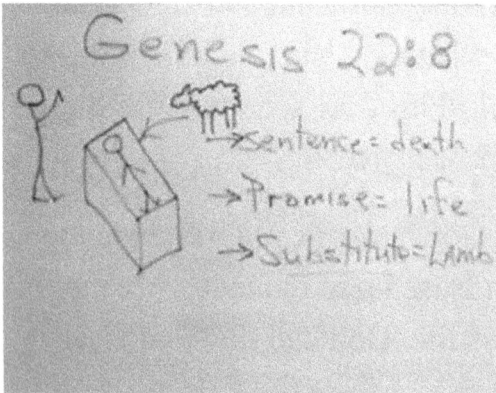

The lamb became the substitute. The lamb had to die so Isaac could live. This became God's way.

The sentence was death. If Isaac died, the promise of life could not happen. Instead, God provided a lamb so that the lamb could die in the place of Isaac so that Isaac could continue to live.

This is exactly what the Gospel message is, my friend. We looked in the last chapter in Romans 6:23. We saw there that the Scriptures tell us that the wages of sin is death.

God has pronounced death upon all of us. Every one of us deserve to die because of our sin.

Yet God promises life. If we are under the sentence of death, how can we live? Can God make a way?

The answer, of course, is yes, He can. The Bible says in Romans 6:23, *"The wages of sin is death,"* you and I have a sentence of death because of our sin.

"But the gift of God is eternal life through Jesus Christ our Lord." That is the promise. Jesus Christ, the Son of God, became the Lamb, the one that would die upon the cross in order that you and I might live.

We have a sentence of death and deserve the very judgment of God. We do not deserve heaven. We deserve hell.

But God has made a promise of eternal life that He would like to give to you and to me. The only way this can take place is the sentence of death must be carried out.

This is the reason that Jesus came into the world, that He might give his life for you and for me.

The good news of the Gospel is that Jesus Christ has become our substitute to pay for our sin that we might be set free from the sentence of death. Jesus Christ was the Lamb of God who died in our place.

Lesson Seven
Are You Passover Safe?
Exodus 12:21-23

Are you Passover safe? What is the story of the Passover in the Bible all about? That is what we want to look at in this lesson.

It is important is to know the Word of God and know what God has for you. He has an answer for your life. He has a purpose for your life and it all begins with having a relationship with Him.

Jacob and all his family had moved to the nation of Egypt. They had gone there because of famine, and they were living there for over 400 years. Finally, a new king came up who did not know anything about the history of the Jewish people.

He thought maybe because they were foreigners that they could not be trusted, so he turned them into slaves. When he did that, the Jewish people began to cry out to God and ask for deliverance.

God raised up a man by the name of Moses. He prepared to lead his people out of the land. But the king of the land of Egypt, the Pharaoh, had determined that he did not want them to go.

Although they had gotten prepared to go and God had told them to go, the king said, "You may not go."

God prepared several judgments for the nation of Egypt. These judgments were so the king of the land would decide to let the people go.

The final judgment is the judgment of the Passover. Here is what the Bible says in Exodus 12:21-23:

"Then Moses called for all the elders of Israel, and said unto them, Draw out and take you a lamb according to your families, and kill the passover.

And ye shall take a bunch of hyssop, and dip it in the blood that is in the bason, and strike the lintel and the two side posts with the blood that is in the bason; and none of you shall go out at the door of his house until the morning.

For the LORD will pass through to smite the Egyptians; and when he seeth the blood upon the lintel, and on the two side posts, the LORD will pass over the door, and will not suffer the destroyer to come in unto your houses to smite you."

This is what God ordered the Jewish people to do in order that they might miss the judgment that was coming. God said that what they needed to prepare for this day and this time of judgment that was coming on the land of Egypt.

God said that the firstborn son in every family of the Egyptians was going to die on the night of the Passover.

But God had instructions for the Jewish people so their firstborn son would be protected and not be killed.

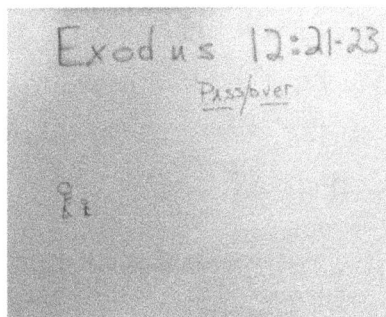

39

God told the Jewish people, "I want you to kill a lamb, and catch the blood of the lamb in a basin.

Then I want you to take that blood, and I want you to apply it on the door of your house."

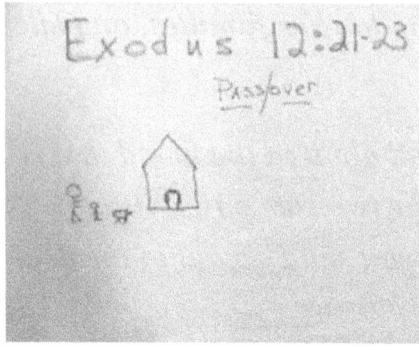

They were to put the blood on the lintel, which is the top part of the door, and on the two side posts of the front door of their house where they lived.

Then God said, "When I pass through the land on the night of the Passover, I will see the blood on the lintel and the two side posts of your house, and I will pass over your house. I will not come in and destroy your firstborn child, because the Lamb has already been killed and the blood has been applied."

The name *Passover* is important. God wanted to *pass over* the homes of the Jewish people if they obeyed what God told them to do.

He called it the Passover before it ever happened. God wanted to pass over the judgment for the Jewish people.

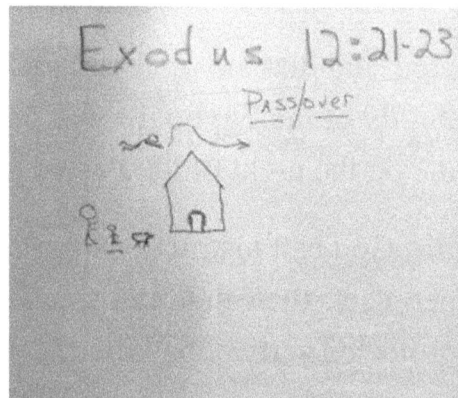

God had specific instructions for the Passover lamb that was chosen. The lamb had to be clean and spotless. It had to be without blemish or disease. It had to be large enough to feed the whole family.

This lamb then, after being chosen, was to be killed. The lamb must die.

You can imagine a young man, a young child, asking the question, "Daddy, why must my lamb die?"

The father said, "It is the order of God. This lamb must die, son, so that you can live."

The death of that lamb would be the substitute. The lamb would be the substitute or take the place of the child so the child would not have to die.

But the death of the lamb alone was not enough. The blood must be applied. The blood must be on the doorposts and on the lintel.

If the blood was not there, there would be no deliverance. But if they chose and killed the lamb the way God said, and applied the blood, then they would be safe. That is the story of the Passover.

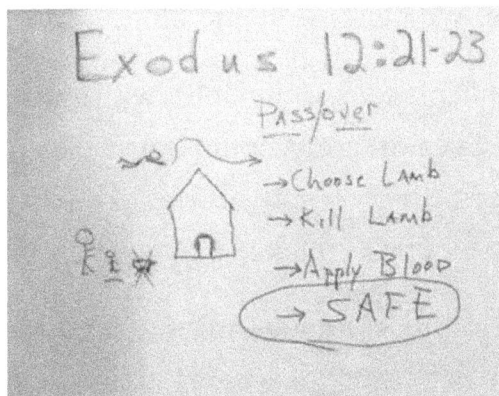

In the New Testament, John the Baptist introduced Jesus in John 1:29. As Jesus was walking towards him, he said to the Jewish people, *"Behold the Lamb of God, which taketh away the sin of the world."*

Every Jewish person listening to John that day would think back to the time of the Passover. They would remember that this lamb must be chosen, this lamb must be killed, but also the blood of that lamb must be applied.

Now Jesus is the Passover lamb. He was sent by God, chosen by God, and qualified by God to be able to be the Lamb that would die in your place and mine so that we would not have to die for our sin.

He died upon the cross of Calvary. He was killed, and God put Him there in order that you and I might be set free. His blood was shed, but the blood must be applied in your life.

If you and I do not receive Jesus as our Savior, if we do not turn in repentance from our sin and in faith to Jesus Christ, we will not be safe. We must apply the blood.

The Bible tells us in Hebrews 10 that the blood of bulls and of goats and even of lambs could never take away sin. The lamb did not take away the sin. It only served as a picture of Jesus Christ who would come and die to take away sin.

Therefore, we do not offer animal sacrifices today. The final sacrifice that God accepts is Jesus Christ. He has already died for you and for me. His death makes it possible for you to be saved from the penalty of sin, but you must apply the blood.

I hope this lesson will be a great encouragement to you and a reminder that you must prepare by applying the blood of Jesus Christ to your life so that you can be safe from the judgment.

Lesson Eight
You Need THIS Miracle
Ephesians 2:1-5

Ephesians 2:1-5 explains to us a miracle from the Word of God that we all need. It says, *"And you hath he quickened, who were dead in trespasses and sins;*

Wherein in time past ye walked according to the course of this world, according to the prince of the power of the air, the spirit that now worketh in the children of disobedience:

Among whom also we all had our conversation in times past in the lusts of our flesh, fulfilling the desires of the flesh and of the mind; and were by nature the children of wrath, even as others.

But God, who is rich in mercy, for his great love wherewith he loved us,

Even when we were dead in sins, hath quickened us together with Christ, (by grace ye are saved;)."

In verse one, God tells us that we were dead. What does God mean when he says you were dead?

We know it is not talking about physical death because you are still alive. You are not in a physical grave.

God is talking about spiritual death. You are cut off from Almighty God.

There is a barrier that is between you and God that keeps you from being able to have a relationship and communication with the God of heaven.

God is in heaven, and He desires a relationship with the people that He has created.

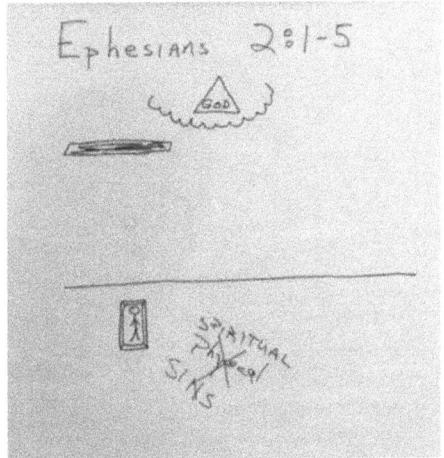

The truth is that you and I are dead in those trespasses and sins. The sins have kept us from God. They are like a barrier that keep us from having a relationship with Him.

Then God talks in verse two about how we walked in times past. He says we walked *"according to the course of this world."* In other words, the way the world goes, that's how we went.

We also listened to the prince of the power of the air, which is Satan himself. He is the spirit that works in the children of disobedience.

The Satan spirit, the devil himself works in us. In other words, we are under Satan's control. Satan is telling us how to live, and we do not even realize that we are being controlled by him.

This is how every man starts off life. He starts off in sin. He starts off spiritually dead in his sins, cut off from God.

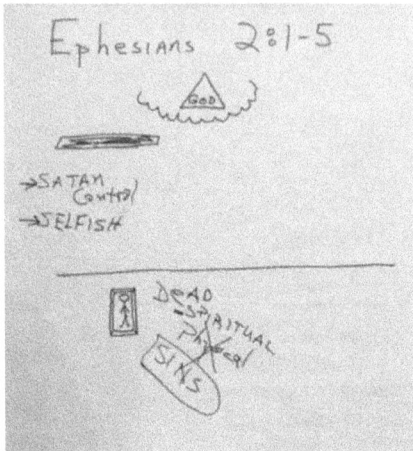

He begins life with Satan in control. Satan is leading him around, and that man or that woman does not even realize that they are being controlled by Satan.

Then in verse three, it says, *"Among whom also we all had our conversation in times past."*

Conversation means the way we live. He says we lived *"in the lusts of our flesh."* In other words, doing what we desired, doing wrong lustful things.

In the next verse, God says that we also obey *"the desires of the flesh and of the mind."* We are not only under Satan's control, but we are a very selfish people.

Satan has taken hold of us, and we are dead spiritually, unable to get the help from God that we need because we are sold our sins. We are bound in our sins.

But that is not where God leaves us. God sees our helpless condition and He offers hope.

In verse one, God says these believers had been quickened. That means to be made alive.

Then in verse 5 God says that we were once dead in sins, past tense, but now we have been quickened together with Christ.

46

Christ had quickened these believers. That is the miracle that you and I need.

Without this miracle, we are cut off from God, out of fellowship with Him, without help from God, and having no relationship with Him at all.

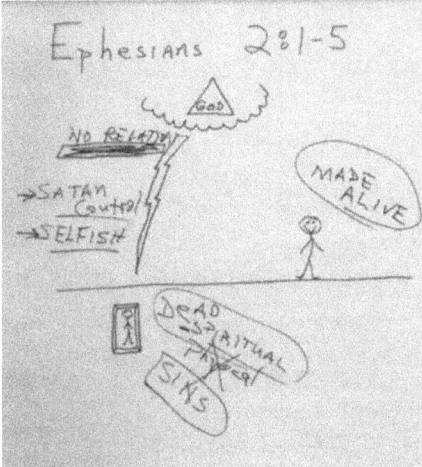

We need a miracle to bring us into life. That is exactly what God promises to do in Jesus Christ. He says, *"And you hath he quickened."*

Those who believe in Jesus Christ been taken from dead in sins spiritually to alive in Jesus Christ.

This is not true of every person. It is only true of those who have come to know this miracle that God offers in Jesus Christ.

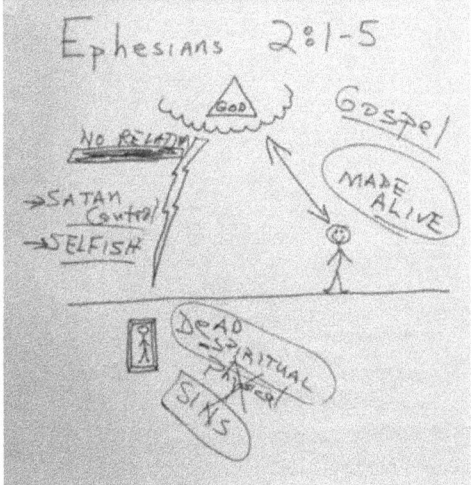

This is what the Gospel is all about, and that is why the gospel is so important. Only what Jesus Christ has done for us can make us alive before God, so that we have this relationship with God.

We can talk with Him and He can direct us. We can be taken out of the control of Satan and put under the control of Jesus Christ.

We do not have to live a selfish life. We can live for God, and we can live in a way that is pleasing to God.

You and I are dead, and we must be quickened. The question is, have you been made alive? Have you been quickened?

This is what the Bible talks about when it says, You must be born again. You must be brought back to life from being dead in your sins. That is the gospel message.

The answers are not found in a preacher. The answers are not found in a church. The answers are found in the Word of God.

God has told us these things so that we can know how to be made alive and put back into a right relationship with Him.

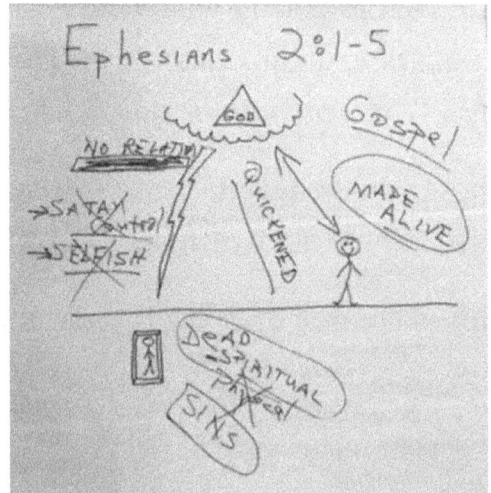

Lesson Nine
Can You Obey a Command If You Do Not Know What It Is?
1 Corinthians 15:3-4

I want to ask you a very serious question. Can you obey a command if you do not know what that command is?

Can you obey a command when you do not know what they are asking you to do? The answer, of course, is no.

In 2 Thessalonians 1:8, it says, ***"In flaming fire taking vengeance on them that know not God, and that obey not the Gospel of our Lord Jesus Christ."***

Think about that verse now: *"In flaming fire taking vengeance on them that know not God."*

Who goes into flaming fire? Those who do not know God and that obey not the Gospel of our Lord Jesus Christ. If you do not obey the Gospel, you will find yourself in flaming fire.

That should concern us, and our first question should be: what is the Gospel? That is what we are going to talk about in this chapter.

When I ask people today, "What is the Gospel?" I will get many different answers.

Some would say the Gospel is music. Certainly there is music about the Gospel, but music is not the Gospel. Others would say the

Gospel is the Bible. Well, the Gospel is in the Bible, but all of the Bible is not the Gospel.

You must know what the Gospel is in order to obey it. We are going to talk about what the Gospel is.

You remember in our last chapter that we talked about how God brings us back to life through the new birth. The Bible tells us in Romans 1 that it is the power of the Gospel that saves us.

The power of the Gospel is what brings us back to life. If we do not know what the Gospel is, we cannot be saved.

If we do not know what the Gospel is we cannot be rescued from the flaming fires of hell. The Gospel is absolutely important for us to know.

1 Corinthians 15:1, *"Moreover, brethren, I declare unto you the Gospel which I preached unto you, which also ye have received, and wherein ye stand."*

The Gospel is what Paul preached. This Gospel is what saved people. This Gospel is the message that they stood on. It was their solid rock.

We must know this Gospel.

He goes on to explain it in verse three, where he says, *"For I delivered unto you first of all that which I also received."* Paul did not invent or make up the Gospel. It was given to him.

There are three parts to gospel. Paul lays it out in verses 3 and 4.

"For I delivered unto you first of all that which I also received, how that <u>Christ died for our sins</u> according to the scriptures." That is part one.

"And that <u>He was buried.</u>" That is part two.

"And that <u>He rose again the third day</u> according to the Scriptures." That is part three.

Let's look at this Gospel. **Christ died**. How did He die? He was hung upon a tree. He was hung upon the cross of Calvary.

That cross that Christ hung upon is where He died. This was a real death. He did not just faint. He did not just disappear, He died.

Then the Bible gives us the reason, **He died for our sins**. Not for His own sins, because He had no sin. But He died for our sins.

He did this **according to Scripture**. This becomes very important in understanding what the Gospel is.

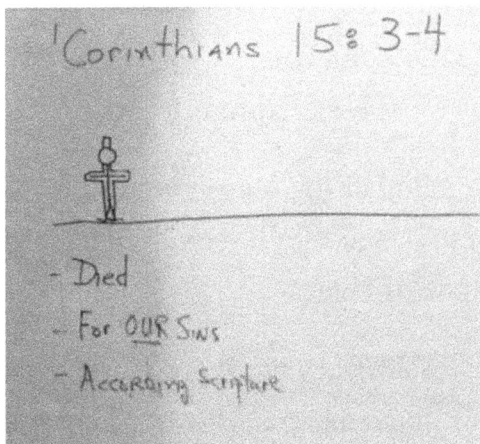

Most people know that Jesus died, but they have no understanding of why He died.

When Jesus went to the cross at Calvary, He said, "No man takes my life from me; I lay it down." No one forced Him to go to that cross; Jesus chose to die.

Why would He choose to die? He was God so He had the power to lay His life down and the power to take it back up again.

Jesus Christ died for our sins. The Bible says the reason we die is because of our own sins. But Jesus died for our sins.

He does not die for His own sins. The reason is because Jesus never committed a sin.

He never spoke wrong. He never acted wrong. He never even thought wrong. Jesus Christ had absolutely no sin.

He died, not for His own sins, but He died for your sins. He died for my sins. He died in our place.

Remember the lesson we did on the lamb that died in the place of the firstborn at the Passover. Then we looked at the lamb that died in the place of Isaac.

The sacrifices are pictures of Jesus Christ who died as a substitute in our place. He paid for our sins so that we can go free and not have to pay for that sin.

He died for our sins, but how did He do it? He did it **according to the Scriptures.**

As we go back in the Old Testament, hundreds of years before Jesus was even born into this world, the Scriptures tell us how the Messiah would die. Jesus died exactly like the Bible had said He would.

He died in fulfillment of those prophecies. When you look at the death of Jesus Christ and you look at the Scriptures of the Old Testament, you say, "Jesus Christ is the one, the only one chosen by God the Father to take away the sins of the world."

He died for us. He died for us according to the Scriptures.

Then the Bible says **He was buried**. This is part two. He was buried. Now what do we mean by buried? He was put in a grave.

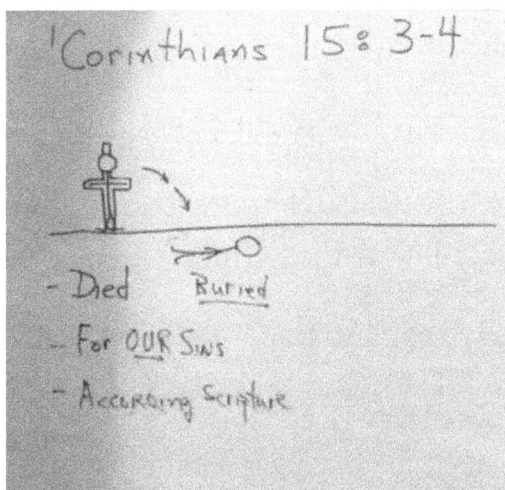

Who do you put in a grave? I have never seen anyone put a loved one that was alive in the grave. We put people in a grave who have already died. Jesus Christ really died and went to the grave.

Jesus Christ was buried because He died, and He was in the grave for three days.

But that is not where the Gospel ends. The Gospel says that Christ died for our sins according to the Scriptures. He was buried.

Corinthians 15: 3-4

- Died   Buried   →Rose again
                         →According Scripture
- For OUR Sins
- According Scripture

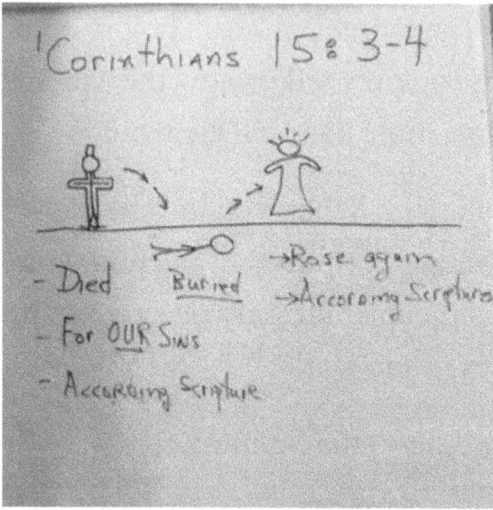

Then it says in verse four, **"He rose again the third day according to the scriptures."**

He rose from the dead. He came back to life. My friend, there has never been another religious leader that has come back to life.

Those who have started their religions have come and gone. Their tombs can still be found.

But Jesus Christ came back out of the grave. His tomb is empty.

He rose again. He came back to life three days later, and He did this according to the Scriptures.

Why is this so important? Because the Bible had promised that He would raise from the dead. No one believed it.

Jesus told His disciples that He was going to die and rise again in three days. But His own disciples did not understand what He was talking about.

They did not believe that He was literally going to raise from the dead, but that is exactly what He did.

1 Corinthians chapter 15 goes on to tell us about proof after proof, people who literally saw Jesus Christ in His resurrected body after He rose from the dead. He really was alive.

The word *Gospel* means **good news.** This is the good news. The good news is that Jesus Christ died for our sins, and He did it according to the Scriptures.

He was buried. But He did not stay in the grave because He has power over the grave, and He rose again from the dead.

He rose again according to the Scriptures. He did not stay in the grave.

Here is the truth we must understand: Jesus did not need to die for Himself. He died for you and for me.

He died in our place, and because of His death, He is able to offer us forgiveness of sin.

How do you know that His offer is a good offer, an offer that you can trust? How do you know it is an offer that God Himself will honor?

The answer, Jesus Christ rose again from the dead. No religious leader has ever done that.

He rose from the dead because He Himself did not deserve to die. He died in your place and mine. He offers eternal life to all.

We go back to our question: **Have you obeyed the Gospel?** Now you understand more about what the Gospel is, but do you understand what the command is?

This is the good news. Jesus died in my place. I deserve to die and pay for my sins in hell, but God offers to me eternal life and forgiveness through Jesus Christ.

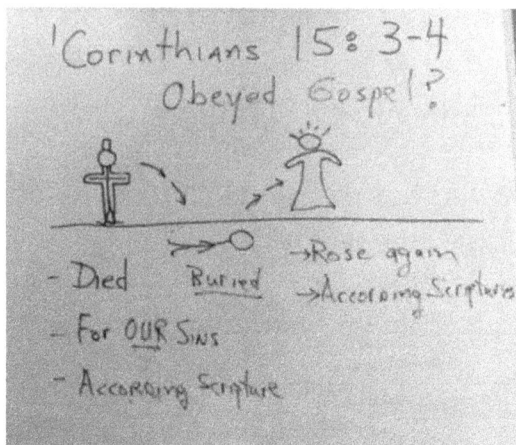

The good news is that Jesus died for our sins according to the Scriptures. He was buried, and He rose again according to the Scriptures.

2 Thessalonians 1:8 tells us there is something we must do to obey the Gospel. What response does God want from us?

Lesson Ten
Your Only Way of Reconciliation with God
Colossians 1:20-23

What is the only way to be reconciled with God?

"And you, that were sometime alienated and enemies in your mind by wicked works, yet now hath he reconciled." (Colossians 1:21)

When God originally made the world, in Genesis chapter one, God said it was good. After He made the land and the sea, He said it was good. After He made the sun and the stars, He said it was good.

After He made the trees and after He made the animals, He said it was good. But when God made man, it was then that God said it was very good.

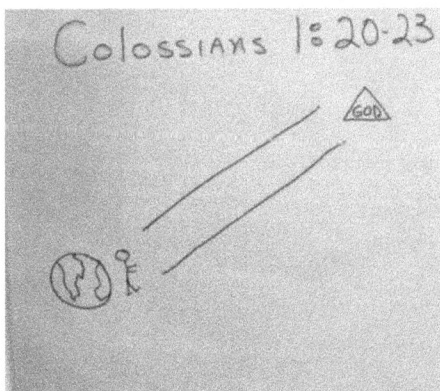

Everything that God made in the world was for the use of man, and God's desire was that there be a relationship between God and man.

That relationship was there until man became alienated, or cut off, from a relationship with God. That happened when Adam and Eve sinned.

At that moment, the relationship between man and God was completely broken.

We ask the question, "Why?" The Bible says in verse 21 that mankind became enemies in their mind.

It all started in the mind of man. As he began to think, his thoughts became wrong thoughts that led him away from God.

His first wicked thought was when he said, "No, God, I will not do that. I will not obey you. I will eat of that one tree in the garden that you said we may not eat."

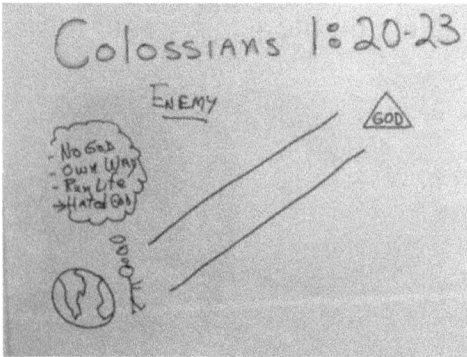

Man chose to say no to God. He then decided that he wanted to do things his own way. He wanted to do what he wanted to do, not what God wanted him to do. That became his choice.

He also decided that he wanted to run his own life. He wanted to make up his own plans for what life should be like instead of listening to what God had for him.

At the end of it all, he hated God. He hated God because God was getting in his way.

This is where a man becomes an atheist. He is not an atheist because there is no evidence that there is a God. He becomes an atheist because he hates God, and he does not want God to exist.

First, we become enemies in our own mind, in our own thinking. But then those thoughts lead to actions.

We choose to do wicked works. Man chooses to lie. That lie becomes the barrier that keeps us from coming into fellowship with Almighty God. That barrier keeps us from being right with God.

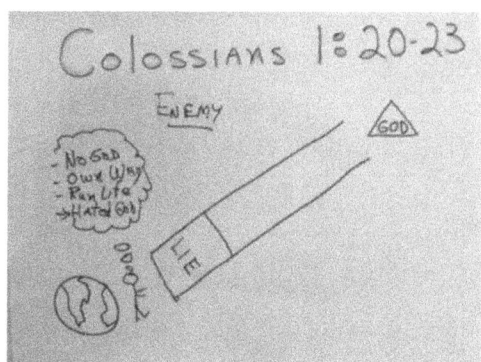

Man chooses to steal and to take that which is not his own. That is what Adam and Eve did in the garden. They stole of that one tree that God said they were not to eat from.

People today take things that do not belong to them, and that becomes a barrier in their relationship with God.

As we begin to blame others for our problems and for our own sin, then anger turns into hatred towards others, just like Cain.

Cain killed his own brother, not because his brother Abel had done anything wrong. God had accepted the sacrifice of Abel, but God had not accepted Cain's sacrifice. That anger turned into hatred, and that hatred turned into murder.

People are also filled with lust and sexual impurity. Jesus warned us about sexual sin. It is all around us. and we all struggle with this sin.

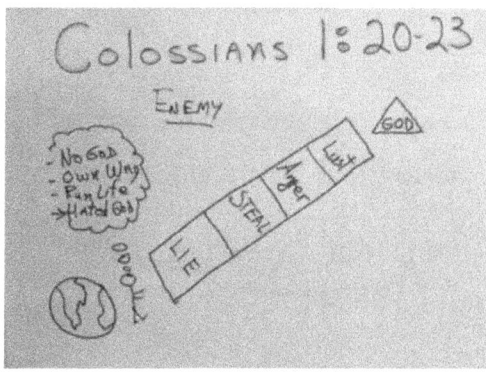

All of these things and many, many others become the barriers that keep us from having a relationship with the God of Heaven.

We ask ourselves, "Where do we find hope? We have been cut off." Some people have decided that God wants nothing to do with them.

They think God does not care about them, so they have chosen instead to live a life apart from God.

They say there is no hope. Then they begin to lie about God. They begin to say that God does not care about them. They believe lies instead of the truth.

God says in Jeremiah 29:11, *"I know the thoughts that I think toward you, saith the LORD, thoughts of peace, and not of evil, to give you an expected end."*

When God looks at man, He sees man with all of his wrong thoughts. He sees the things that block our way from fellowship with Him.

God says He wants to find a way to open up and restore fellowship with mankind. God's desire is to reconcile us, to make us right with Him.

To **reconcile** means to bring us back together with Him. How does God do that? He does that by way of the cross of Jesus Christ.

We talked in the last lesson about the Gospel of Jesus Christ. Jesus died for us; He died for our sins. He died in our place.

Ours sins demand a judgment. They demand that you and I pay for this sin. But God knew we could not pay for our own sin.

So God sent Jesus Christ into the world that He might go to the cross in our place. Jesus Christ died on the cross to pay for our sin.

This is why the Bible says in Colossians 1:22, *"In the body of his flesh through death, to present you holy and unblameable and unreproveable in his sight."*

Jesus Christ died on the cross of Calvary. On that cross, Jesus Christ shed His blood. He covered our sins by His blood, opening up the way to God, so that you and I can have a relationship with Him.

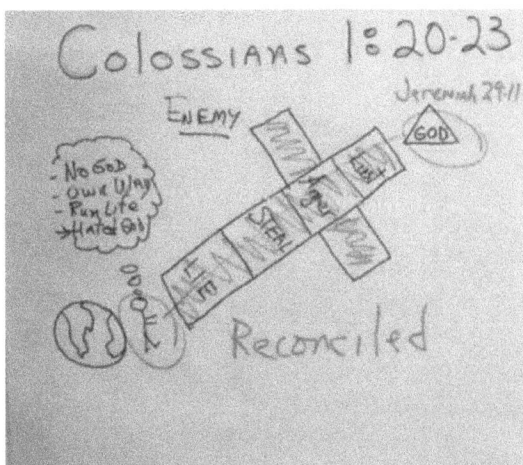

He did that by way of His own blood, by way of His own death. He made it possible that you and I could be reconciled to God, brought back together with God.

We can have a relationship with Almighty God by way of the cross of Jesus Christ. This is why the death of Christ becomes so very necessary. If Christ did not die in our place, you and I could not be reconciled, brought back to God.

If Christ did not die on the cross of Calvary, the possibility of mankind being made right with God would be completely gone. We would deserve only the judgment of Almighty God.

Yes, we can go from an enemy of God to reconciled by way of the cross of Jesus Christ.

Lesson Eleven
Can the Gospel Be This Simple?
2 Corinthians 5:21

Can the Gospel really be that simple? Yes, it is. The Gospel is simple.

2 Corinthians 5:21, *"For he hath made him to be sin for us, who knew no sin; that we might be made the righteousness of God in him."*

In this short verse, God gives us a simple explanation of what the Gospel is all about. He hath made Him to be sin for us.

He is referring to God. *Him* is referring to Jesus Christ. So we could read it like this: God made Jesus Christ to be sin for us.

Jesus Christ is the One who came into the world to die for our sins. He was God in the flesh who came without sin.

His whole life on this earth was lived without sin. He never spoke a sin. He never committed a sin. He never even thought about doing sin. He never had a thought that was sin. He never broke one of the Father's commandments.

He lived a perfect life, total perfection. This is Jesus Christ. He is the only One who has ever lived this way. God made Jesus Christ to be sin for us.

All of us are born into this world as sinners. The Bible says, **"All have sinned and come short of the glory of God."**

We are all guilty of breaking the law of God. We all bear our own weight of sin and deserve the judgment of God.

Here is the very center of what the Gospel is all about. This perfect Jesus took the sin that you and I have upon Himself.

This is reason that Jesus Christ went to the cross of Calvary. There on that cross, He died that your sins and mine might be paid for.

His death on the cross paid for our sin. The Bible says that everyone that hangs upon the cross is cursed.

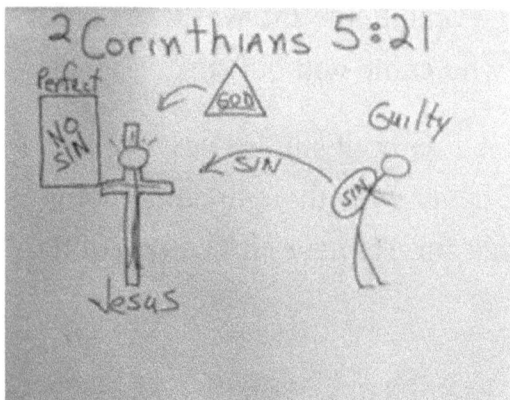

Jesus Christ hung upon the cross, not because of His own sin, but because of our sin. He became a curse for us when He paid for our sins.

We are guilty before Almighty God. Someone must pay for that sin. Jesus Christ paid for the sins of every person that is born into this world.

"He hath made him to be sin for us who knew no sin." Jesus had no sin. Yet He took our sins upon Himself so He could pay the penalty for that sin.

Why did He do that? **"That we might be made the righteousness of God."**

God took the righteousness and perfectness of Jesus and put that upon us. When He did that, it canceled out our sin debt so that we would not have to be guilty before Almighty God.

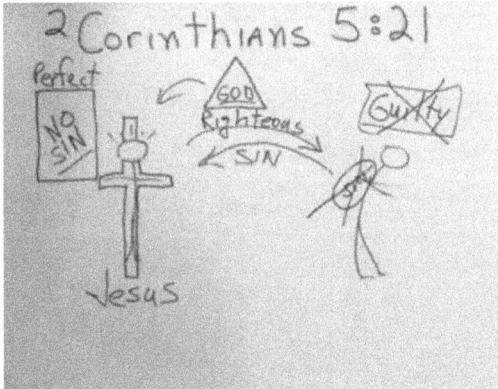

Jesus Christ traded places with us. God took our sin and put it on Jesus so that He could take the righteousness of Jesus Christ and put it upon us.

The Bible is very clear that when a man dies, he will either go up to heaven to be with God, or he will go down to hell and be in punishment for all of eternity.

Jesus Christ has suffered for the sin of all men. He has paid for that sin in order that we might be made righteous in Jesus Christ. But that does not mean that every person goes to heaven when they die.

Some will go to hell; some will go to heaven. My question for you is this: what makes the difference?

God has done everything He needs to do, but there is a response that God asks for from us that we might be made right with God.

Then this transaction of our sin put upon Christ and the righteousness of Christ put upon us can take place.

Your response to the gospel message will determine whether you go to heaven or whether you go to hell. We will look at the response God wants from us in the next chapter.

Lesson Twelve
Do You Have Bible Repentance?
Acts 20:21 and 1 Thessalonians 1:9

We have seen that the Gospel is the death of Christ for our sins, His burial, and His resurrection, according to the Scriptures. Now we want to look at this question: what is our response supposed to be?

It is a two-part response. The first part of that response has to do with repentance. Do you have Bible repentance?

There are many ideas about what repentance is. Many people talk about repentance, but do not repent the Bible way.

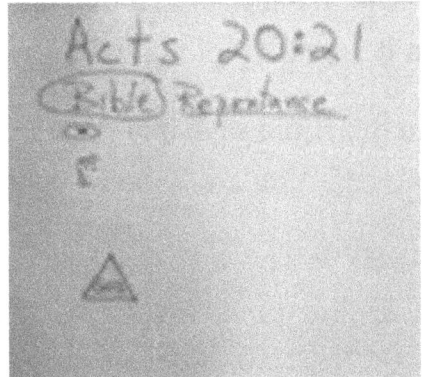

We need to understand how God sees repentance, because God is not going to work on our standards. God wants us to approach Him the Bible way.

God wants us to come to Him the right way so He can receive us and forgive us. We want to look at what the Bible teaches about this important subject.

In Acts chapter 20, the Apostle Paul was speaking. He was talking about his ministry and what he had preached.

"Testifying both to the Jews, and also to the Greeks, repentance toward God, and faith toward our Lord Jesus Christ." (Acts 20:21)

Paul preached to both Jews and to Gentiles. He was not just concerned about one race of people, but he wanted all people to hear the message.

He preached that people must repent. He called it repentance toward God. What is Bible repentance?

First, true Bible repentance **changes the way we look at sin**. When we look at our sin, we usually think we are not bad sinners. We think we are really good people who sometimes might do a few things wrong. We like to call our sin "a mistake," something we did wrong, but it is really not that bad.

But the Bible says that if you say you have no sin, you are deceiving yourself. You are lying to yourself.

The Bible says also that you do not have the truth in you. You are not seeing things the way God sees them.

This is what repentance begins with. We must see our sin for what it is, how serious it is. It is so serious that Jesus Christ had to die to pay for our sins. That is how serious sin is.

You are a sinner. I am a sinner. It is not that we make a few mistakes, but that our hearts are wicked. Our life is filled with this selfishness and willingness to just live for ourselves.

We also need to see the Savior. We must see Jesus Christ for who He is,

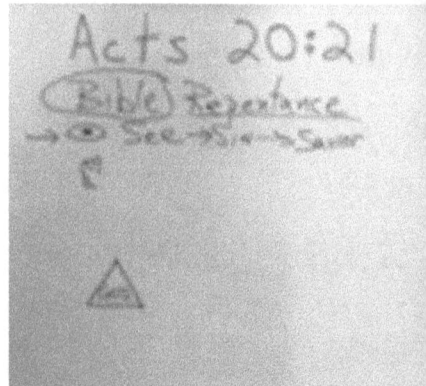

the Holy One who came and died for our sins on the cross. He paid for our sin.

If there was some way that I could do enough good works to earn my way into heaven, then Jesus Christ would not have needed to die. His death was necessary because our sin was so serious before God.

Second, Bible repentance **brings Godly sorrow.** Why are you sorry when you sin? Why are you sorry when you do wrong? Usually, we are sorry because we get caught.

When you get caught doing wrong, someone sees you are doing wrong. You feel bad because of being caught. You feel worldly sorrow. You are sorry you got caught.

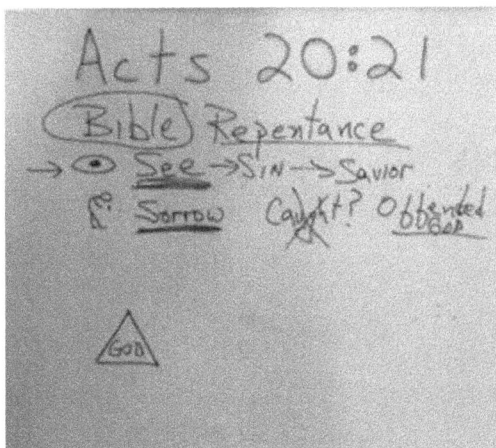

If you had gotten away with it without being seen, you would have gone on living. If nobody found out that you did it, you would have just gone on your way and ignored it.

But when we have Bible repentance, our sorrow is not just about being caught. Our sorrow comes because we recognize that we have offended God.

Acts 20:21 says we need **repentance toward God.** That is because God is the one we have offended.

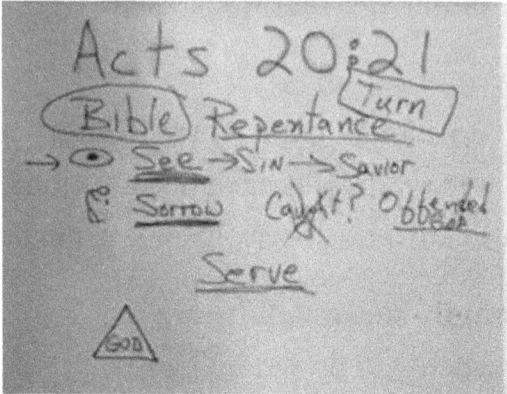

That is what Bible repentance is all about. We see that we have wronged God, and it bothers us in our heart. We are deeply sorry.

Godly sorrow is also a sorrow that causes us to wish to change, to be different than what we are. We know we cannot change ourselves because now we see how bad our sin is, but we want desperately to be different.

That is why Job said in Job 42:6, *"I repent in dust and ashes."* Job got down in the dirt. He poured the dirt and ashes upon his head because he felt so bad about his sin.

He had sinned against God. He had wronged God. He dishonored the name of God. He had not followed through and been the kind of person that God wanted him to be.

This is where you and I live. We need to see our sin. We need to have a new sorrow that no longer is worried about getting caught, but about offending God. We know that God is the one that is most important.

Third, Bible repentance **changes the person that we serve.** We no longer want to serve self or idols. Now we want to serve God.

In 1 Thessalonians 1:9, the Bible says, *"For they themselves shew of us what manner of entering in we had unto you, and how ye turned to God from idols to serve the living and true God."*

Paul says, when we came to Thessalonica to preach to you, we preached the Gospel. And when preach the Gospel, you repented.

No, he does not use the word repent, but he talks about turning from idols to God.

That is repentance. Repentance is turning. It is a change that takes place.

Paul said they turned from idols. Idols are that which we serve. It is anything or anyone that we put before God in our life.

What are you serving? Who are you serving?

Eve in the Garden of Eden saw that the fruit on the forbidden tree was pleasant, and that it was to be desired to make one wise. She chose to eat the fruit that God had forbidden.

When she ate the fruit on that tree, she was serving herself. She was more concerned about herself than she was about God.

She had turned her back on God, and she was serving, living for, and honoring herself.

Her attitude was, "Let me do what I want, instead of what God wants." And that is what she did. Then, she turned and offered that fruit to Adam.

When Adam looked at that fruit, he not only saw the fruit, but he understood what he was doing. Adam chose the fruit, because he knew if he did not choose the fruit, he could lose his wife. Adam wanted his wife more than he wanted God, so he chose the fruit.

Abel offered the sacrifice that God ordered, but Cain offered the sacrifice that he wanted to offer. He ignored God's instructions about the kind of offering to bring.

He had his own religion that he loved more than he loved God. He wanted to serve and worship his way instead of the Bible way. Because of that, Cain turned his back on God.

Who are you serving? Everybody serves **themselves**. We are most concerned about what will benefit me, instead of what does God want.

It is not unusual for people to want a wife or a girlfriend or a husband or a boyfriend, and they are more concerned about their **relationships** than they are about God.

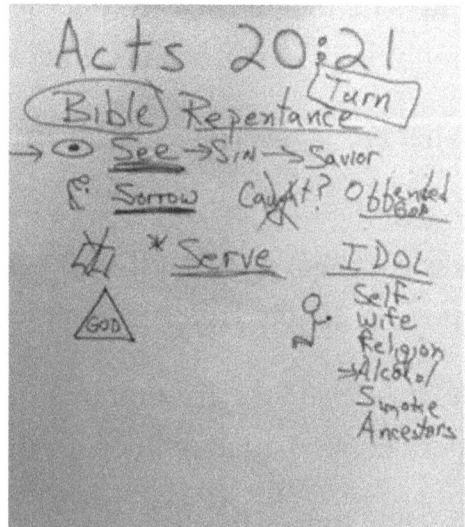

Acts 20:21
Bible Repentance Turn
→ ◉ See → Sin → Savior
Sorrow Caught? Offended
* Serve IDOL
GOD Self
Wife
Religion
→Alcohol
Smoke
Ancestors

They are not concerned about doing what is right before God. This is what the Bible calls an idol.

Some serve their **religion**. They are more concerned about the religion than serving God. They are not concerned about what God says is right in the Bible.

They are more concerned about having a religion that they like, so they ignore the Bible and they serve their religion. By doing that, they turn their back on God.

Today, some people will serve **alcohol**. Drinking booze becomes the thing that they love more than God. Some would rather **smoke** than serve God.

Others would rather have their **ancestors**. We should be thankful for those who have gone before us, but they are not God. They are not a god, and they are not the ones that we should worship.

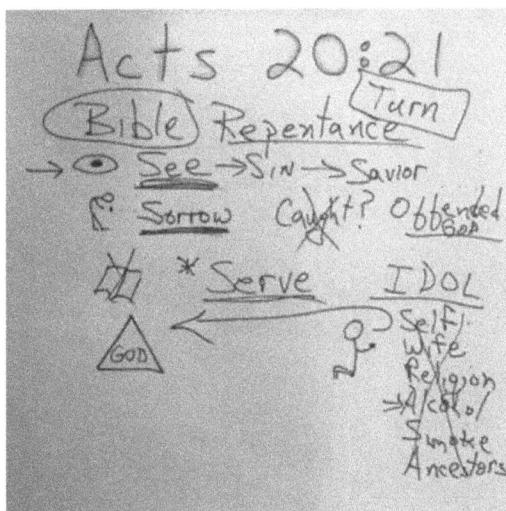

The people at Thessalonica turned from idols, and they turned to God. This is what repentance is. It is turning from the idols and turning to God.

Repentance is a change.

It is a change in the way we see our sin and the Savior.

It is a change in our sorrow.

It is a change in our thinking.

It is a change in the person that we are serving. We turn from everything else and turn to serve God.

We no longer are just worried about ourselves. We are concerned about offending God. We no longer serve ourselves.

We no longer serve others. We no longer serve our own ways. Instead, we want to serve God. This is what Bible repentance is.

My question is, do you have Bible repentance?

Lesson Thirteen
Responding to God's Grace in Real Faith
Acts 20:21 and Ephesians 2:8-9

What is the response to the Gospel that you and I should have? In this lesson we are going to talk about the response of faith.

God tells us how to respond to the Gospel in Acts 20:21. The Gospel is the death of Christ for our sins. He was then buried, and He rose again from the dead.

God did all of that for us. Yet, the Bible tells us that you and I have a response that we need to make. God wants us to respond to the truth of His Word.

In Acts 20:21, Paul said that he was *"testifying both to the Jews, and also to the Greeks, repentance toward God, and faith toward our Lord Jesus Christ."*

Paul did not leave anybody out. It did not matter whether you were Jew or whether you were Gentile. Both groups of people needed to hear the Gospel.

The first part of our response is that we must repent towards God. We talked about that in our last lesson. If your repentance is wrong, your faith will be of no value.

The second part of our response is **"Faith towards our Lord Jesus Christ."** Let me illustrate this truth with you with a story from back in 1859.

In Canada, a man by the name of The Great Blondin was known as an acrobat because he can walk on high wires. In 1859, he went to Niagara Falls.

Niagara Falls is a little smaller than Victoria Falls in Zimbabwe, but nevertheless it is a very large waterfall. The water comes rushing along and then goes down over the falls.

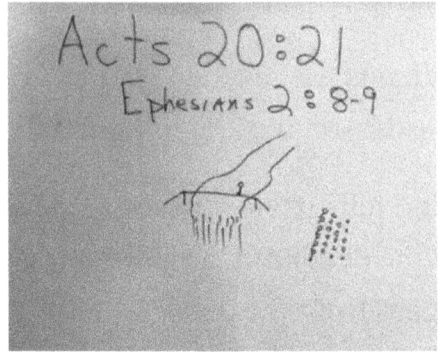

Mr. Blondin strung himself a high wire from Canada to the United States over Niagara Falls. The United States was on one side. Canada was on the other side.

He then announced for everyone to come on a certain day to see him walk across the wire over the waterfall. On that day, he got on the wire, he walked part way out over the waterfall, and then he turned around and came back.

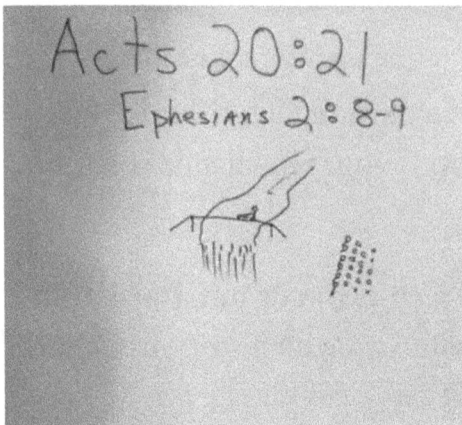

The people that were there that day began to clap and applaud. They were so excited to see him do that.

He then asked them, "Do you think I can do walk on the wire while pushing a wheelbarrow?"

They all cheered and said, "Yes, you can do that."

So, he pushed the wheelbarrow out part way on the wire over the waterfall, and he turned around and came back. Again, the people shouted and cheered.

Then, he said, "Do you believe that I can put a man in that wheelbarrow, and I can push him out there?"

And their answer was, "Yes, you can do that."

But do you know the next question that he asked?

He asked, **"Which one of you will get in the wheelbarrow?"**

Everybody in the crowd took a step back, and they said, "Not me. No, not me. Not me. I do not want to get in the wheelbarrow."

They **said** that they believed that he could do it, but they were not **willing to risk their own life** to get in the wheelbarrow and try it. Finally, his campaign manager stepped out of the crowd, and he said, "I will go."

And he did. He got in the wheelbarrow, and The Great Blondin walked him out on the wire, turned the wheelbarrow around and brought him back again. And everybody cheered.

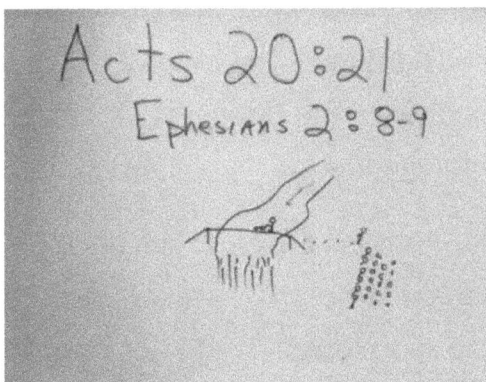

What should be our response to the Gospel message? The Bible says that we need to respond by faith in the Lord Jesus Christ.

Faith means **belief,** but Bible belief is not just thinking something is true. Bible belief is much more than believing something is true.

Bible belief is **being willing to trust in Jesus Christ.** It means that you are willing to risk your life and eternity on the truth of what God says in His Word. That is Bible faith.

The Bible, for instance, says that the devil believes, but he trembles. He is not changed. He does not have Bible faith.

Bible faith is more than believing something. It is trusting God. Think for a moment what this Bible verse says.

Our faith is towards our Lord Jesus Christ. What did Jesus do for you and me? He died for our sins. He died in our place, according to the Scriptures.

What else did He do? He was buried. You only bury a dead man. Then He raised from the dead.

If this does not make sense to you, read the chapter again that talks about what the Gospel is. You must understand the Gospel to be born again.

Our faith must be in what Jesus Christ has done for us. Our faith is in His works. We do not have faith in our works, but in the works of Jesus.

If we want to be born again and

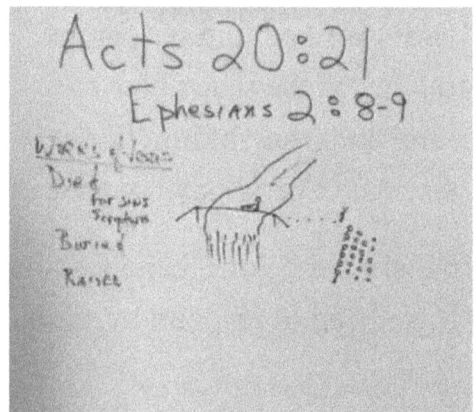

be a child of God, we must have faith towards our Lord Jesus Christ.

Imagine this picture for a moment: You are on one side of the waterfall, and it is certain destruction to be there.

The Bible says all men have been born in sin. All have sinned, and the wages of that sin (what we deserve because of our sin) is death. We deserve to spend eternity in hell paying for our sin.

But God offers to us eternal life. He says, "This is what I have done for you. But you must be willing to let me take you to the other side of the waterfall, and the only way you can get there is by faith."

The Bible says in Ephesians 2:8-9, *"For by grace are ye saved through faith; and that not of yourselves: it is the gift of God: Not of works, lest any man should boast."*

Listen to what God says. How are you saved? How are you brought from the side of certain death to eternal life to salvation in Jesus Christ?

How does this take place? Ir is done by grace. It is done by what God does for you, and He did that in Jesus Christ.

By grace you are saved, but it is through faith. You must have the belief to get in the wheelbarrow. You must have the faith to trust God to save you by the death of Jesus Christ.

You must be willing to put yourself in God's care. You cannot just say, "I think it might be true." You must be willing to trust totally in what Jesus Christ did for you.

"For by grace are ye saved through faith; and that not of yourselves: it is the gift of God. Not of works, lest any man should boast."

This is something that only God can do for you. Why? Because it is not by works.

It is not what you do that makes you right with God. You cannot walk across to get on the other side for eternal life. You must trust God to take you to the other side.

I encourage you to put your faith in Jesus Christ alone, to turn your back on your own works and recognize that what you do can never make you right with God.

You must trust in Jesus Christ and turn from your own sins.

Repent (turn from your own sins) and have faith (trust) in Jesus Christ alone.

Lesson Fourteen
Have You Come TO Salvation?
1 Timothy 2:4; 2 Peter 3:9; John 6:37

We are going to talk in this chapter about coming to salvation. Have you come to Bible salvation?

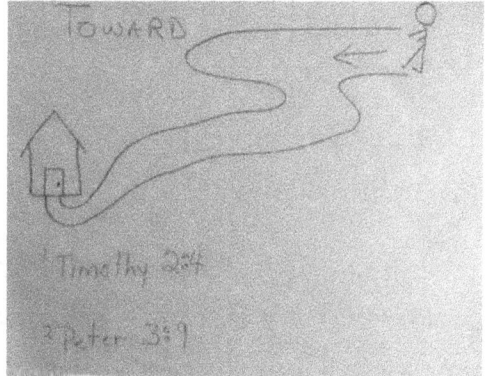

You have said it before, "I am coming to your house now," but that does not mean that you have arrived. It means you have started on your way.

You are coming toward the house. But coming toward the house is not the same as being at the house.

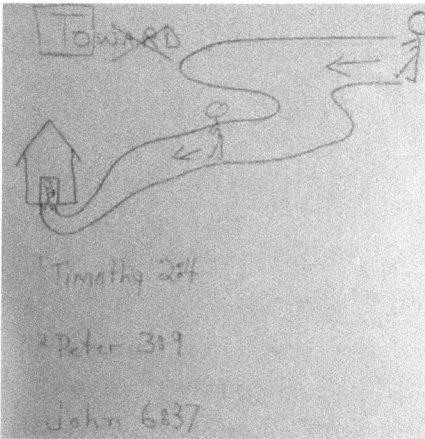

But some would say, "No, no, I am at the house. I have arrived, and I am entering into the house."

These people have come to the house, not just toward the house.

Have you come to Bible salvation? We need to be born again the Bible way.

This is not just coming towards the Bible or just starting to understand things about the Bible. We must come all the way to

Bible salvation. We must come to Jesus Christ for the salvation that He offers.

Have you come to Christ? Have you come to Bible salvation? We are going to look at three questions.

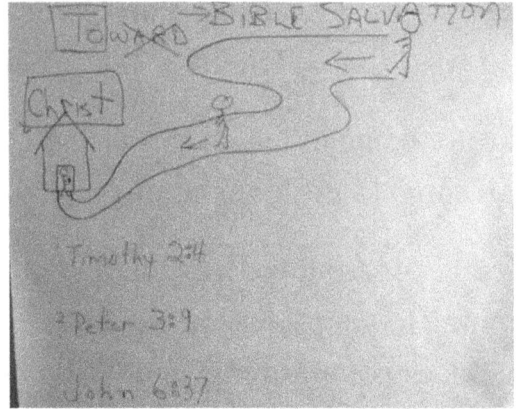

First, **have you come to the knowledge of the truth?**

First Timothy 2:4, *"This is good and acceptable in the sight of God our Savior; Who will have all men to be saved, and to come unto the knowledge of the truth."*

It does not matter who you are or where you live. God wants all men to be saved.

God also wants all men to come unto the knowledge of the truth. This is more than just understanding that the Bible is the Word of God.

The Bible says you must come to the knowledge of the truth. What is the truth? The truth is found in the Word of God.

You do not have to know everything in the Bible to be born again. But there are some things in the Bible that you must know to be born again the Bible way.

You must know **about your sin**. You must know about the price of your sin. You must know the consequences of you sin. Because of your sin you deserve the wages of that sin, which is death.

You must also understand that **you cannot save yourself.** Your good works are not enough to get you into heaven.

You must also understand **who Jesus Christ is.** He is God who came in the flesh. He was born into this world like you and me in order that He might pay for our sin.

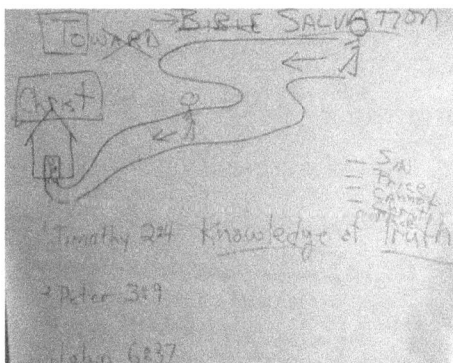

You must also understand that **He died in your place.** He died as your substitute to pay for your sin. You must come to Him to be born again.

These are things that you must know and understand. So, have you come to the knowledge of truth?

You may say, "I went to church," but that is not the knowledge of the truth.

You may say, "I know the Bible is the Word of God," but that is not the knowledge of the truth.

You may say, "I know that Jesus is the Savior," but that alone is not the knowledge of the truth.

You must understand that you are a sinner, that there is a price you need to pay.

You must understand that you cannot save yourself, that Jesus Christ died to pay for your sin, and He is the Savior of the world.

You must understand that Jesus Christ has taken your place as your substitute, and you must come to Him.

You must know and understand these truths. Have you come to the knowledge of the truth?

Second, **have you come to repentance?**

Second Peter 3:9: *"The Lord is not slack concerning his promise, as some men count slackness; but is longsuffering to usward, not willing that any should perish, but that all should come to repentance."*

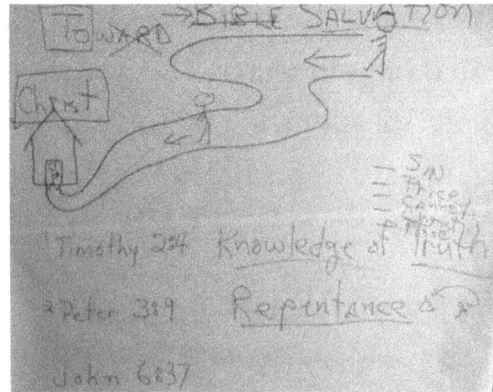

God does not make promises that He does not keep. He does not make a promise and then come short of fulfilling it. But God is taking time to fulfill His promise to us.

Why? Because He is **"not willing that any should perish, but that all should come to repentance."**

Peter is talking about is the promise that Jesus Christ will come back to this earth. He is going to come back, and He is going to reign.

One day Jesus Christ will be the King of kings on this Earth. That day has not come yet, but He is coming.

Why is he waiting? Why is it so long? Because He's not willing that any should perish, but that all men should come to repentance.

He wants us to come, not towards repentance, but God wants us to come to repentance.

What is repentance? We talked about repentance in one of our previous lessons.

Repentance is when we see we are worshipping wrong gods, and we turn away from those false gods and turn to the God of the Bible.

We turn away from the idols that we have erected in our life. We turn from the idols that we worship in our life and the things that we live for.

We turn away from them, and we turn instead to the God of the Bible to worship and honor and love Him alone.

That is what repentance is. It is a turning from our idols and a turning to God.

Have you turned away from your idols, the things that you live for, the things you put before God in your life?

Maybe it is alcohol. Maybe it is sex. Maybe it is a relationship, a wife, a husband, or a child. Maybe it is just having your own way in life.

Maybe it is ancestors. Maybe it is your false religion that you believe in, a religion that is not in agreement with the Word of God.

My friend, you need to come to the Word of God. You need to come to the God of the Bible, and worship Him and Him alone.

That is what repentance is. It is a turning away from your own ways. Have you come to repentance?

True repentance is not just coming towards repentance, making some changes here or there in your life.

No. You must come to place where you say, "I will turn from my idols and worship only the true God of the Bible. I will trust in Him alone."

Third, **have you come to Jesus Christ**?

John 6:37: *"All that the Father giveth me shall come to me; and him that cometh to me I will in no wise cast out."*

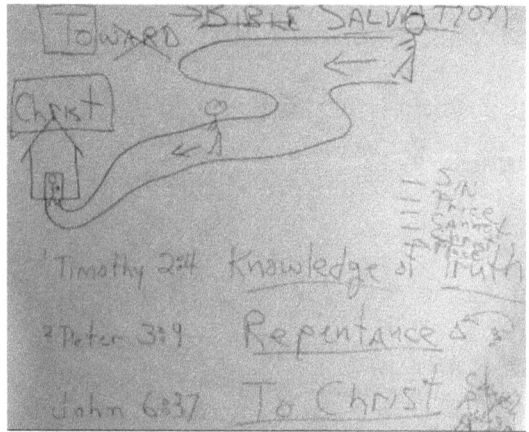

God wants us to come to Jesus Christ. It must be Jesus Christ that we come to.

No, it is not a church we must come to. It is not a religion. None of those will ever save us.

It is not a preacher. It is not a prophet. It is not an apostle. It is not a pastor.

We must come to Jesus Christ, for He alone is the Savior of the world. He alone is the One that can save us from our sins.

Bible salvation, my friend, is not coming **towards** the knowledge of the truth. It is not coming **towards** repentance. It is not coming **towards** Christ.

It is coming **to** the knowledge of that truth, the truth found in the Word of God about how to be born again.

It is coming **to** repentance and turning from our sin.

It is coming **to** the person of Christ, the Jesus Christ of the Bible, trusting in Him alone and believing in Him alone as the only way of salvation.

My question for you is: Have you come to the knowledge of the truth? Have you come to repentance? Have you come to Christ?

Have you come to salvation?

Life is full of struggles, challenges and problems.

God has the answers to life itself,
but ONLY if you know HIM.

The free Gospel Lessons will help you
come to have a relationship with the
God who made you.

You can get the first lesson in the Gospel

Lessons by contacting Bible Baptist Ministries
On Whatsapp: +27-711-222706
On Facebook:
http://www.Facebook.com/BibleBapMin
By Email: BibleStudyAfrica@gmail.com

www.ingramcontent.com/pod-product-compliance
Lightning Source LLC
Chambersburg PA
CBHW051637050426
42443CB00025B/432